Love Came Down

Written by BETHAN LYCETT
Illustrated by HANNAH STOUT

10

God made the world,
God loved the world,
all that you can see,
from mountains high
to oceans deep,
and rivers running free.

He made the plants of all designs,
from flowers to mighty trees,
bearing fruit, or nuts, or seeds,
and nectar for the bees.

Animals of every kind:
fish and birds and mammals,
frogs and lizards, slugs and bugs,
crocodiles and camels.

God made people last of all
to be His special friends.
He loved them, saying, "Very good!"
But that was not the end.

The people did not listen to the
things that God had said,
ignoring Him and doing things
that made Him sad instead.

These bad things (we call them sin)
were getting in the way,
but people couldn't fix them,
and there was a price to pay.

So God sent His only Son to Earth,
a special baby boy...

Jesus, born in Bethlehem,
to bring the world true joy.

Angels told
about His birth
to shepherds
on a hill,
"Go find Him
in a manger bed."
The shepherds said,
"We will!"

The wise men
travelled from the East,
really, really far,
bringing gifts
to worship Him,
and following a star.

God sent Jesus
just for us.
He had a
special plan...

to make our
friendship right again,
like when the
world began.

The story didn't just end there.
Jesus grew up too.
He didn't stay a little boy.
He had a job to do.

Healing people where He went:
the blind, the lame, the sick.
His power amazed all those He met.
It wasn't just a trick.

Jesus lived a perfect life,
like no one had before.
He loved and cared for people
who others would ignore.

Jesus died for everyone
at Easter long ago.
He paid for all the wrong we've done,
God's perfect love to show.

EASTER

Do you believe
in Jesus,
that He really
lived and died,
then came to life
and went to Heaven
to sit at God's
right side?

If we trust that He has paid
for all the wrong we've done,
He will forgive all those bad things,
each and every one.

We can ask Him to forgive us
and live for Him each day.
His Spirit helps us follow Him
in every single way.

Did you guess that's not the end?
Jesus lives forever!
His friends will go to Heaven one day
and worship Him together!

"God loved the world so much
that he gave his one and only Son
so that whoever believes in him